No act of kindness,
no matter how small,

is ever wasted.

–Aesop

Butterfly Wings

an illustrated journal

or more deeply engrossed in anything than when we are playing. – Charles Schaefer

We are never more fully alive, more completely ourselves,

He who
experiences
the unity of life
sees his own Self
in all beings,
and all beings
in his own Self,
and looks on
everything
with an impartial eye.

– Buddha

Keep on beginning and failing. Each time you fail, start all over again, and you will grow stronger until you have accomplished a purpose - not the one you began with perhaps, but one you'll be glad to remember. –Anne Sullivan

Believe there are no limits but the sky.   —Cervantes

things in incredible ways. —Alexander Volkov

Your journey never ends. Life has a way of changing

Since you get more joy out of giving joy to others, you should put a good deal of thought into the happiness that you are able to give.

-Eleanor Roosevelt

The universe is full of magical things, patiently waiting for our wits to grow sharper.   —Eden Philpotts

Nothing can bring you peace but yourself.   – Emerson

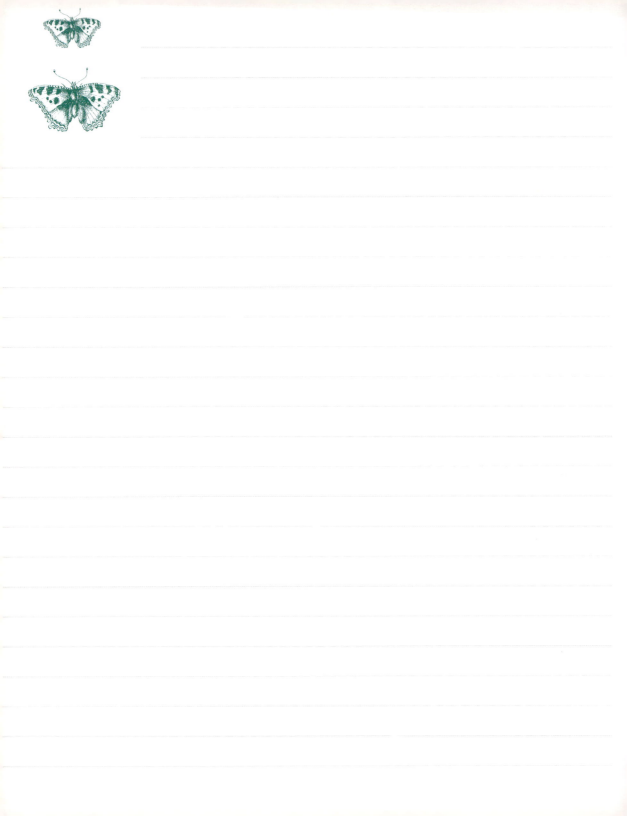

If nothing ever changed there would be no butterflies.

Giving
opens
the
way
for
receiving.

- Florence Scovel Shinn

There is no instinct like that of the heart. — Byron

Faith is the strength by which a shattered world shall emerge into the light.   —Helen Keller

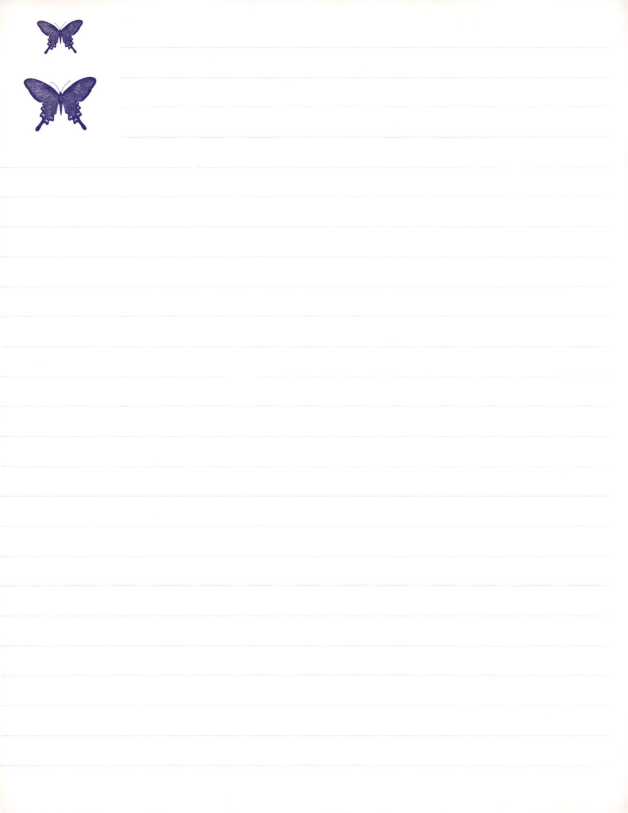

Logic will get you from A to B. Imagination will take you everywhere. —Einstein

and has time enough.   -Tagore

The butterfly counts not months but moments

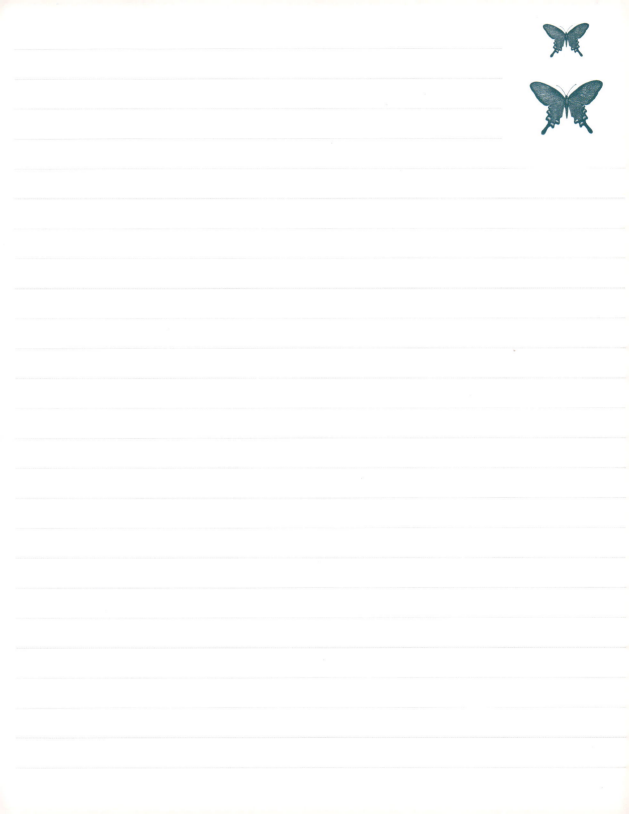

"Just living is not enough," said the butterfly, "one must have sunshine, freedom and a little flower." ~Hans Christian Anderson

They seemed to come suddenly upon happiness as if they had surprised a butterfly in the winter woods.

~Edith Wharton

We delight in the beauty of the butterfly,
but rarely admit the changes it has gone through
to achieve that beauty.

~Maya Angelou

I do
not know
whether
I was
then
a man
dreaming
I was
a butterfly,
or whether
I am
now
a butterfly
dreaming
I am
a man.

~Chuang Tzu

We live in this world when we love it. ~Rabindranath Tagore

Love is like a butterfly,

it goes where it pleases
and it pleases where it goes.

so much taller than they are. Whoever would partake of all good things must understand how to be small at times. ~Nietzsche

We must remain as close to the flowers, the grass, and the butterflies as the child is who is not yet

The butterfly is a flying flower, the flower a tethered butterfly. ~Ponce Denis Ecouchard Lebrun

We
are
like
butterflies
who
flutter
for
a day
and
think
it is
forever.

~Carl Sagan

The moment one gives close attention to any thing, even a blade of grass, it becomes a mysterious, awesome, indescribably magnificent world in itself

-Henry Mill

Everyday is a journey, and the journey itself is home.   -Basho

No act of kindness, no matter how small, is ever wasted. –Aesop

We do not see things as they are. We see them as we are.   —The Talmud

Until we see what we are, we cannot take the steps to become what we shall be.   —Charlotte Gilman

but which, if you will sit down quietly, may alight upon you.   ~Nathaniel Hawthorne

Happiness is a butterfly, which when pursued, is always just beyond your grasp,

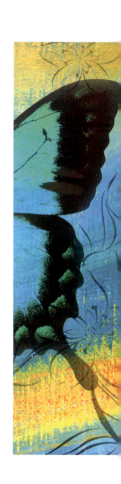

It is good to have an end to journey towards; but it is the journey that matters in the end.

—Ursula LeGuin

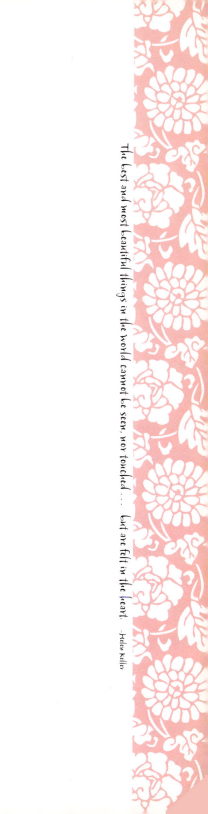

The best and most beautiful things in the world cannot be seen, nor touched … but are felt in the heart. —Helen Keller

We should not be impatient, but we should confidently obey the eternal rhythm. —Kazantzakis

Cynthia Louden merges photography and painting, the concrete and the obscure, and the known and the unknown to create a wonderfully heightened sense of reality.

Copyright © 2007. Published by Brush Dance
All rights reserved.

No part of this book may be reproduced or transmitted in any form or by any means, electronic or mechanical, including photocopying, recording, or by any information storage and retrieval system, without written permission from the publisher.

All artwork by Cynthia Louden
Book design by Liz Kalloch